FIRST 15 LESSONS

VOICE

by Elaine Schmidt

POP SINGERS' EDITION

Includes Audio & Video Access

2	**LESSON 1** Full-Body Singing		18	**LESSON 9** Music Literacy
4	**LESSON 2** Breathing		20	**LESSON 10**
6	**LESSON 3** Finding Your Voice			
8	**LESSON 4** Vocal Warm-Ups I		24	**LESSON 12** Working on a Song
10	**LESSON 5** The Vocal Break		26	**LESSON 13** Dealing with Nerves
12	**LESSON 6** Caring for Your Voice		28	**LESSON 14** Making a Song Your Own
14	**LESSON 7** Vocal Warm-Ups II		30	**LESSON 15** Rules and Tools
16	**LESSON 8** Diction			

PLAYBACK+
Speed · Pitch · Balance · Loop

To access audio, video, and extra content visit:
www.halleonard.com/mylibrary

7905-8645-6172-9488

ISBN 978-1-5400-1384-2

HAL·LEONARD®
7777 W. BLUEMOUND RD. P.O. BOX 13819 MILWAUKEE, WI 53213

Visit Hal Leonard Online at
www.halleonard.com

Full-Body Singing

Although a singer's vocal folds, or vocal cords, create the sound an audience hears when the singer performs, that tiny portion of the singer's body is only part of the equation that allows them to sing. Singing is a full-body endeavor, from the way a singer stands or sits to the way they breathe, the way they shape words, and how much tension they carry in their neck, shoulders, and back.

Singers do a series of physical and vocal warm-ups before each practice session, rehearsal, and performance, all of which are designed to make their voices and bodies work at peak efficiency for singing, and to protect them from singing-related injuries that can crimp a vocal style, or even cause permanent damage to a singing voice.

Stretch to Relax

Video 1

Watch as the singer in Video 1 demonstrates some of the basic body warm-ups you can use to shed physical tension before you begin to sing.

It may seem, at first glance, that it will take a great deal of time to get through these physical warm-ups, but it really won't. Once you have gotten comfortable with each warm-up, you will move through them seamlessly, just as you would with a familiar yoga routine. The warm-ups are extremely valuable in warding off tension-related issues, so it's worth the time it will take to do them every day.

Stand (Sit) Up Straight!

Good posture is the starting point for good singing. For an object lesson on posture and breathing, stand up, put your feet close together and slouch forward as much as your body will let you. Now, without straightening up at all, try taking a deep breath and singing a lovely resonant note. It didn't work well, did it? Try doing the same thing while slumped forward in a chair. Even worse!

Video 2

Watch the singer in Video 2 for a look at ensuring good singing posture when standing.

Don't lock your knees. Doing so can make you feel light-headed, or even cause you to faint. Keep your knees straight, but not rigidly locked. Keeping your weight on the balls of your feet, as opposed to on your heels, can help keep you from locking your knees.

There will be situations in which you're going to find yourself singing while seated. Although you can't center your hips and shoulders above your feet while seated in a chair, you can still use good posture. When singing from a seated position, always sit up straight, with both feet flat on the floor and making sure you're not resting your back on the back of the chair. Take note that crossing your legs while singing pulls your spine out of alignment and tugs as the muscles of your back and abdomen – none of which makes for good breathing.

Video 3

Watch the singer in Video 3 for a look at good singing posture when sitting. If you are going to be doing a lot of singing while sitting, prepare by spending some of your practice time doing warm-ups and breathing exercises while sitting.

Making Some Sound

Listen as the singer in Track 1 sings the warm-up written below. After you've heard it a couple of times, sing along to get the hang of the warm-up, then try it with the piano in Track 2. Always breathe deeply and silently, relaxing your throat as you inhale and thinking of filling your entire body cavity with air. If it helps to place your hand on your stomach to feel the depth of your breathing, feel free.

1 & 2

Listen to the demo of "Danny Boy" on Track 3, paying attention to the long, even-sounding phrases the singer creates. Take deep, relaxed breaths as you begin working with the accompaniment in Track 4, striving for long, evenly supported phrases.

3 & 4

Danny Boy

Words by Frederick Edward Weatherly
Traditional Irish Folk Melody

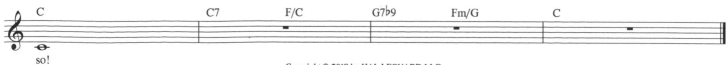

Breathing

As stated in Lesson 1, singing with a full, free, natural sound is a full-body endeavor. Although your vocal cords reside in your throat, everything from your sinuses to your feet is involved when you begin to sing. Whether you're standing in front of an audience or sitting in a rehearsal, your posture and body position have as much of an effect on your singing as your diaphragm (the muscle you use to pull air into your body and push it back out again) does.

Video 4

Watch Video 4 for instructions on a three-step warm-up that will energize your breathing and get you ready for your physical and vocal warm-ups and for making a polished vocal sound. This quick warm-up should always be the first step in vocal warm-ups and can be used at any point in your non-singing activities when you need some extra energy.

Video 5

Now that you've gotten your diaphragm working and practiced a few deep breaths, try the relaxed breathing exercise in Video 5 to reinforce what you've learned. This is going to require lying on the floor, so dress appropriately.

When singers talk about singing from the diaphragm, or supporting their sound, they are referring to taking deep, relaxed breaths, just as you did while sprawled out on the floor, and then using that air efficiently and evenly.

Video 6

Watch as the singer in Video 6 performs a warm-up designed to foster a smooth, supported sound. Then listen closely to yourself as you perform this warm-up. You will be making a soft sound, striving to make it smooth.

A silent version of this exercise can be used as a mid-gig breathing tune-up. Moisten your palm and hold your hand, with your palm facing you, about 12 inches from your mouth. Take a deep breath and aim a focused stream of air at the moist spot on your palm. You will able to feel if the air stream is steady or choppy – keep it steady.

The breathing warm-up you just learned can also be used with a sung note, once you have mastered the steady, soft hiss. For that variation on the exercise, replace the hiss with a soft, straight tone (a note without vibrato) in about the middle of your vocal range. Sing on a gentle "hah" sound, sustaining the note as long as is comfortable.

Time to Sing

It's time to put your breathing work to good use! Listen to the singer warming up with five-note scales in Track 5. Sing along with the accompaniment in Track 6, concentrating on deep, relaxed breathing, and on making a full, even sound. In addition to the "mee, may, mah" syllables the singers uses, you may also sing this warm-up with the syllables "vee, vay, vah," and "nee, nay, nah."

 5 & 6

Mee.
May.
Mah.

Now, listen as the singer on Track 7 sings the following octave warm-up. As you perform the warm-up with the accompaniment on Track 8, concentrate on making a clear, even, relaxed sound and create a gentle surge of air as you move to the higher of the two notes.

7 & 8

Mah   mah   mah   mah   mah   mah   mah   mah   mah   mah.

Now that you've thoroughly warmed up your breathing apparatus, sing though "Scarborough Fair," taking care to breathe deeply and make a relaxed, well-supported sound. Breathe as needed when you first begin working on this song, working to breathe only at the beginnings of phrases.

9 & 10

Scarborough Fair

Traditional English

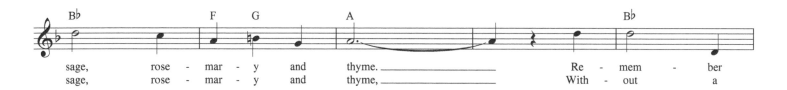

Are   you   go - in'   to   Scar - bor - ough   Fair?   Pars - ley
Have   {him}{her}   make   me   a   cam - bric   shirt,   Pars - ley

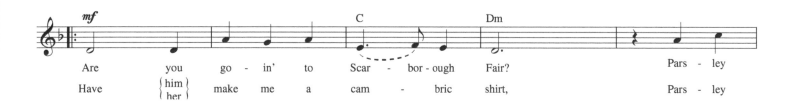

sage,   rose - mar - y   and   thyme. _____   Re - mem - ber
sage,   rose - mar - y   and   thyme, _____   With - out   a

me   to   one   who   lives   there, _____   For   once   {he}{she}
seam   or   fine   nee - dle   work, _____   And   then   {he'll}{she'll}

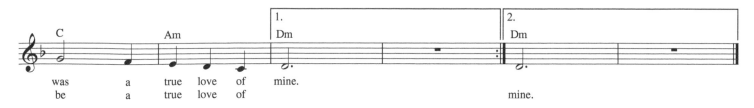

was   a   true   love   of   mine.
be   a   true   love   of   mine.

Finding Your Voice

Think of your friends and family and the fact that each of them has a speaking voice that's uniquely theirs. Most of us know these familiar voices immediately when we hear them. Singing voices are no different. Every singing voice on this planet is unique, thanks to the combination of timbre (tone quality), pitch (whether a voice is high or low), any sort of regional accent, and what sort of treatment (smoking, drinking, shouting) the voice has gotten over the years.

Singing voices may all be distinct, but most fall into one of six broad range categories: soprano, mezzo-soprano, alto, tenor, baritone, or bass. Sopranos are the highest of the female voices while tenors are the highest of the male voices. Mezzo-sopranos and baritones are somewhat lower voices, while altos and basses are the lowest. Although these categories are traditionally used in classical and choral music, they're useful for describing voices in any style of singing. Pop/rock singer Peter Cetera, opera singer Placido Domingo, and jazz singer Mel Tormé are all tenors – wildly different musicians, but all tenors.

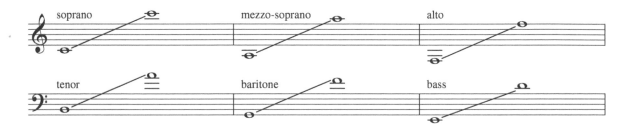

 More important than being able to put the right name to your voice type is knowing how high and how low you can comfortably sing – in other words, knowing your vocal range. Listen to the singers in Track 11 (women) and Track 12 (men) using a range-finding exercise; print a copy of the online PDF from the MyLibrary page. Get a pencil and use the musical examples to determine your vocal range, circling the measure on which you can comfortably begin the exercise and the measure on which you stop singing. (The PDF examples reflect the actual notes heard on the audio tracks.)

 11 Range-finding exercise (women)   **12 Range-finding exercise (men)**

Expanding Your Range

Someone born with a tenor voice can no more become a bass than a short person can become tall. Still, your range will almost certainly expand as you begin singing and practicing regularly. But you can expand your natural range somewhat through careful, steady work with exercises like the one included below.

 13 & 14

Listen to the singer on Track 13 and then sing with the accompaniment on Track 14, doing both the ascending and descending versions of this exercise in a full, supported, *mezzo forte* (medium loud) dynamic. Listen to the piano accompaniment before you sing to choose a starting point that is comfortable for your voice.

As the exercise moves higher or lower, you will begin to feel as though you are reaching slightly for either the highest or lowest notes of the little phrase. Once you feel that stretch, sing just one more repetition of the pattern and then stop. Stretching your range is a slow process.

After a few weeks of repeating this exercise, always starting and stopping on the same pitch, you will find that the notes that were too high or too low have become easy to sing. At that point you can go on in the exercise, stretching your range just a bit more.

You can also work on expanding your range with a song that has a limited range, perhaps an octave or less. "Skye Boat Song," an old Scottish folksong that has become popular in recent years as the theme song for the Starz Network series *Outlander*, has a range of exactly one octave. Using the online *PLAYBACK+* feature, you can try it in several different keys. Pick the one that is easiest for you to sing. As your range expands, you can move to the next higher or lower key.

15 & 16

Skye Boat Song

Words by Robert Louis Stevenson
Traditional Scottish Melody

Vocal Warm-Ups I

Once you've done your basic, physical warm-up, it's time to move on to warming up your voice. Always remember that both body and voice warm-ups are an essential part of maintaining a healthy voice. Singing without warming up is like running without stretching – the likelihood of an injury is too great to take the risk.

First Things First

Singing requires putting the rest of your busy life aside and focusing on both the physical and creative components of making art through sound. Before you begin, turn off your smartphone. Always keep a notebook and a pen or pencil handy when you practice. When stray thoughts intrude on warm-ups or practice sessions, write them down in the notebook and don't think about them again until you're done practicing. Anything you write down while warming up and practicing can be your To-Do List when you're done.

Getting Your Lungs Ready to Work

Air and lots of it is essential to singing well. The following exercises will help you relax and expand your breathing apparatus in preparation for singing. It will also get your diaphragm warmed up and ready to work efficiently. This exercise, performed daily, will gradually expand your lung capacity.

 Video 7

Watch the singer in Video 7 go through a breathing warm-up that will help open your lungs and expand their capacity. Listen to the instructions and try it yourself. In addition to being a helpful warm-up, this exercise can serve as a good stress reliever in your daily life.

Taking air into your lungs is only half of the battle – you also have to be able to control it as you exhale and sing. The following two warm-ups will focus on creating a steady, smooth air stream that will support your sound as you sing.

 Video 8

Watch Video 8. The goal of this warm-up is to produce a gentle, singing sigh, striving to make it smooth. You will often hear other singers doing this warm-up as a relaxing exercise before auditions or in the middle of rehearsals. This is also a good relaxation exercise to insert as needed into your practice sessions.

Singers refer to the following warm-up as a lip roll, lip trill, or lip buzz. It both looks and feels pretty silly. You'll just have to get over that. It's a great way to warm-up all the little muscles of the face that are essential to clear, crisp enunciation in your singing. It also helps in developing the smooth, steady stream of air that's essential to producing a good vocal sound and helps you focus and direct your sound.

To perform a lip roll, take a deep, relaxing breath and push your lips forward. Keeping them relaxed and closed, blow a steady stream of air through them and let them buzz. Do this several times until you can sustain an even buzz for as long as it takes you to finish exhaling. Now hum a pitch and buzz your lips at the same time. No, it's not pretty, but it is effective. Once you've produced a good, humming buzz, sing the following warm-up along, buzzing throughout.

 17 & 18

As you learn "Homeward Bound," by the legendary songwriter Paul Simon, try singing parts of it with a lip-roll to stay relaxed as you practice.

Homeward Bound

Words and Music by Paul Simon

The Vocal Break

All singers have a *chest voice* (think Broadway belt) and a *head voice* (a lighter, less forceful sound). Most singers experience sort of a vocal tripwire between the two registers, or types of singing, called *the break*. You'll know your break when you encounter it – it sounds a bit like an adolescent boy's voice breaking as it begins changing. It's a natural phenomenon. Every singing voice has a break, but it's not the show-stopping obstacle you might think. For some singers, the sound difference between head and chest voice is quite distinct, for others not so much.

 21

Listen to the singers in Track 21 singing over their breaks. Imitate what you hear, starting low in your range with your hand on your chest to feel the vibrations of chest voice singing and moving up the scale until your voice flips into head voice. You will feel and hear the difference instantly.

All singers have to decide how to handle their break. Without a break in their voices, yodelers wouldn't be able to make their trademark sound (listen to Franzl Lang on YouTube) and singers like Patsy Cline (listen to her recording of "Crazy") would have been pretty bland. But not every song or style of music requires an obvious break in the voice. In fact, most don't.

Smoothing the Break

 22

Listen to the singers in Track 22 as they sing over their breaks smoothly and gracefully in "Skye Boat Song." (The music is on page 7.) There is no magic pill to make the break disappear. You simply need to know it exists and practice making a smooth transition over the break whenever a song requires that you move from chest voice to head voice. Sing along with the singers in this example and find the point at which your voice "breaks."

 23

In Track 23, you'll hear the same scales and singers as Track 21. Listen as they sing seamlessly across the vocal break. Regardless of how different your chest and head voices sound when you begin working on your break, you have to try and smooth them out so that they are as alike as possible. Listen again to Track 23 and then sing along, making the transition from your own chest voice to head voice as smooth as possible.

Take a Deep Breath

Relaxing and supporting your sound with air will make an enormous difference in smoothing over the break in your voice. Don't force, or blast air through your throat to make sound in any part of your register. Understand exactly where your own break lies and use steady, even support and a relaxed throat and jaw as you approach it.

Whenever your break presents a problem in a song, begin a few notes below your break and sing over it – gently, gracefully, and with lots of air support. Notice that, in tracks 22 and 23, the singers are performing in a relaxed, natural fashion and using lots of steady air.

Singing Over the Break

The break in your voice is never going to go away. There will always be a point at which you have to switch from one area of the voice to the other in ascending or descending lines. This exercise, which works well as a daily warm-up, is designed to help you sing over that break smoothly and easily, minimizing the sound differences between your head voice and chest voice.

On Track 24, the singers use the exercise below to smooth over their breaks. Listen to the piano accompaniment on Track 25 and pick a starting point that places your break in about the middle of the scale. Sing along with accompaniment from that point, starting in your chest voice and striving to make the notes on either side of your break sound as much alike as possible. Stand tall, plant your feet, keep your knees unlocked and take a good, relaxed breath before you begin. Repeat this exercise a couple of times, moving up or down by half steps with the accompaniment, until your break is no longer near the middle of the scale.

 24 & 25

Caring for Your Voice

As you get more serious about singing, you're going to come up with questions that can't be answered in the pages of a book. You're going to need a teacher – and possibly a coach – to help you refine your sound and style.

The difference between a teacher and a vocal coach is one of generalities and specifics. A teacher will help you develop good vocal technique that will keep your voice strong and healthy, and will teach you repertoire, or songs, designed to help you shape and polish your voice. Your relationship with your teacher will probably be a long one, meeting every week or two for several years.

A vocal coach, on the other hand, is someone who can help you prepare for a specific audition or a performance and can tell you what's working or not working from a performing/auditioning/stylistic standpoint. A coach will polish specific pieces, will know what the "hot" audition songs are at the moment, and will help you get ready for events/specific situations. But a coach will not guide you through the long, careful process of developing a solid vocal technique.

You can go to a vocal coach a couple of times before an audition and then not return for months. Many professional singers use both teachers and coaches throughout their careers, getting different things from both of them. They will also use different coaches for different types of music. As you're starting out, you should find a teacher who has a good reputation for turning out solid singers.

Living a Singer's Life

Do:

- Get plenty of sleep.

- Stay hydrated. Drink plenty of water and warm liquids (herbal teas with no milk or cream). If you live in a very dry climate, a humidifier will help keep your vocal cords and sinuses from drying out at home, particularly in months when the furnace or air conditioning is running.

- Keep throat lozenges handy. If your throat is feeling irritated, it's better for your voice to drink lots of liquids and let a throat lozenge dissolve in your mouth than to clear your throat repeatedly and make it more irritated.

- Wear a scarf or muffler if it's cold out and try not to talk or inhale through your mouth when the air is terribly cold. Cold air can make your throat raw and irritated and your muscles tense.

Don't:

- Scream and shout at sporting events or in loud bars.

- Smoke, or hang out in smoky places.

- Tackle sanding projects without a mask.

- Inhale the fumes from household cleaners.

- Try a new lipstick on the day of a gig or audition, as some lipsticks can cause scratchy throat or an allergic reaction.

- Clear your throat. It just makes those delicate tissues more irritated.

- Sing if your throat is sore or irritated. In fact, try not to talk under such conditions.

- Eat dairy products before singing.

- Wear perfume. You may want to ask your accompanist or anyone you're performing with to avoid perfumes too, as they can irritate the throat.

If You're Sick:

- Drink lots of warm liquids and clear broths. (Tea and chicken soup. Mom was right!)
- Rest. This means stay at home and don't talk on the phone.
- Don't try to sing while you're feeling ill. Aside from further irritating a sore throat and prolonging your down time, the fact that you don't feel well means you won't be breathing or supporting your voice well either.
- When you start singing again, go slowly and pay attention to the way you sound and feel.
- You may not be able to sing while you're sick, but you can listen. Have your teacher or your accompanist make a recording of the piano parts of the songs you're working on. Listen and count, getting used to the way your lines fit into the accompaniment.
- Listen critically to recordings of the songs you're working on. Listen to your favorite recordings of the songs and those recordings you don't care for. Work on putting your likes and dislikes about them in words. Be specific. By determining what speaks to you in other singers' performances, and what doesn't, you are developing your own taste and style.

Vocal Warm-Ups II

A good vocal warm-up wakes up your breathing apparatus, gets your voice limbered up, and touches on many of the skills you need to sing with a beautiful sound and without injuring your voice. A good warm-up routine may look like a lot of work, when it's written out on paper, but it won't take up as much time to get through as you might think. Once you are familiar and comfortable with them, the warm-ups will flow smoothly from one to the next, much like elements of a good yoga workout.

Limbering Up for Clear Diction

Listen to the singer on Track 26 performing a diction warm-up on a major scale, placing a word on each note of the scale. Once you join in, and later, when you sing this warm-up with the accompaniment on Track 27, focus on crisp, clean diction. Think of standing at the front of a large room and singing the words clearly enough to be understood by someone standing at the back of the room. Each set of words works different parts of speech.

26 & 27

Many nanny meaning leaning kneeling railing raining real.
Chair care tar par patty tacky chatty catchy.
Bar grill deal Jill good dead jade bread.
Very measure zero thy treasure mere Zen then.
Who how flew show three see shy thigh.

Flexibility

There is as old adage in theater circles that you should "never let them see you sweat." It also applies to singing. You should never let your audience know that something you're singing is difficult. This means keeping a look of stress or worry off your face and having the vocal flexibility and agility to handle tricky passages.

The next few exercises will work on flexibility – the ability to move cleanly and accurately through running and leaping passages. This first exercise should be sung quickly and lightly, both articulated and slurred. Listen to the singer in Track 28. Join in when you feel comfortable. Then sing it on your own with the accompaniment in Track 29.

28 & 29

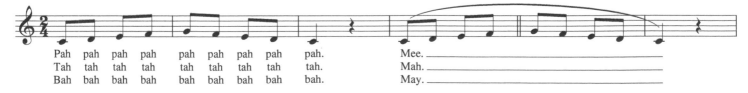

Accurate Intervals

This flexibility exercise works on small intervals: the major second (whole step) and minor second (half step). It's easy to overshoot these intervals, particularly when they occur in fast phrases. Listen to the singer on Track 30 performing these warm-ups slowly at first, then a bit faster. Sing along when you're comfortable. This exercise provides a road map for all your vocal practice. As a rule, if you can't sing a passage accurately and cleanly at a slow tempo, you certainly can't sing it accurately and cleanly at a fast tempo. Always start out slowly and speed up your tempo once you can sing the piece easily at a slow tempo. Use the accompaniment in Track 31.

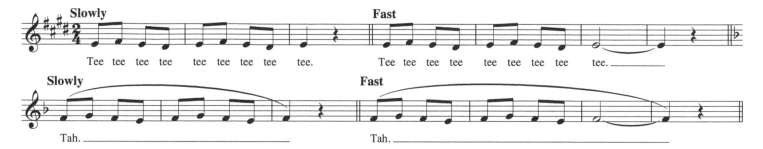

Tee tee tee tee tee tee tee tee tee.

Tee tee tee tee tee tee tee tee tee.____

Tah._____

Tah._____

American songwriter Stephen Collins Foster (1826-1864) penned "Hard Times Come Again No More" in the 1850s. Listen to the performance on Track 32. When you begin working on the song with accompaniment (Track 33), start by singing with the syllables you used earlier in this lesson. Add the lyrics when you are comfortable with the melody and rhythms.

 32 & 33

Hard Times Come Again No More

Words and Music by Stephen C. Foster

Let us pause in life's pleas - ures and count its man - y tears while we all sup sor - row with the poor. There's a song that will lin - ger for - ev - er in our ears. Oh! hard times, come a - gain no more. 'Tis the song, the sigh of the wea - ry: hard times, hard times come a - gain no more. Man - y days you have lin - gered a - round my cab - in door; Oh! hard times, come a - gain no more.

Diction

Have you ever wondered why the Beatles sounded so British when they spoke, but so American when they sang? Diction. They sang with pronunciations that are known as "Casual American." Pronunciation – technically, "diction" – is also the reason that a country singer from the Bronx sounds like a country singer from Nashville when he or she sings and someone singing opera sounds like a native of whatever language they happen to be singing in at any given moment.

In addition to the melody you're singing, diction lets your audience hear the words, allowing you to communicate with both. The following exercises are designed to sharpen your diction and increase your awareness of shaping consonants and vowels well and projecting lyrics with your sound. They make a great addition to your daily singing warm-ups, but many of them can be done anytime – in the shower, while waiting at a stoplight, etc.

Listen to the singer in Track 34, singing this exercise slowly, at a moderately full (or *mezzo forte*) volume. Repeat this exercise with the following syllables: mee, may, mah, moe, moo. Then change the first consonant to v, w, f, h, n, s, th, r, j, l. The goal is to make your vowels warm and open, to make your consonants clear (but not hard or disruptive), and to make the moves from one note to the next smooth and fluid.

 34

Mee _____
Zee _____
Nee _____
See _____

Tongue Twisters

Consonants can become an issue in fast passages. Here are several good tongue twisters for working on consonant clarity. One gem of a tongue twister is "Peter Piper:"

Peter Piper picked a peck of pickled peppers.
A peck of pickled peppers, Peter Piper picked.
If Peter Piper picked a peck of pickled peppers,
Where's the peck of pickled peppers Peter Piper picked?

The following phrases are tongue twisters. Repeat each several times, slowly, without pausing. Really move your lips and tongue to get the clearest enunciation possible. As they become comfortable when done slowly, begin to pick up the pace. Always speed up gradually, taking it just a little faster and mastering the phrase at the new speed before trying to speed it up any more.

- Blue Buick, Black Buick.
- Seth at Sainsbury's sells thick socks.
- Real race winners rarely want red wine right away!
- Tie twine to three tree twigs.
- Five frantic frogs fled from fifty fierce fishes.
- Eleven benevolent elephants.
- Weary real rear wheel.
- Double bubble. Triple trouble.

- Three free fleas flew through three tree's leaves.
- Three Plymouth sleuths thwart Luther's slithering.
- Thin grippy thick slippery.
- Fresh French flies fried fritters.
- Toy boat. Toy boat.
- Black background. Brown background.
- Six slimy snails sailed silently.

Sung Twisters

Listen as the singers demonstrate how to use the following sung twisters. Try it yourself, using the sing-along tracks.

35 & 36 — A prop-er cop-per cof-fee pot. A

37 & 38 — Three gray geese in green fields graz-ing.

39 & 40 — We sure-ly shall see the sun shine soon.

41 & 42 — Wil-lie's real rear wheel, Wil-lie's real rear wheel.

43 & 44 — A-round the rug-ged rocks the rag-ged ras-cals ran. A-

Listen to the demo of "I Ain't Got Nobody" in Track 45. Pay close attention to the words as you practice this song. Work on the lyrics without the music and work on the music without the lyrics, making sure you master both.

45 & 46

I Ain't Got Nobody (And Nobody Cares For Me)

Words by Roger Graham
Music by Spencer Williams and Dave Peyton

Music Literacy

Reading music, an essential skill for anyone who wants to make music, is no longer taught in many schools. If you are one of the numerous people who has not yet learned to read music, take heart: the Internet is littered with sites and apps that teach music reading. But until you're up to speed, here are few easy tools to help you learn your music and speak the language.

All notes have names. Here is a map of the piano keyboard:

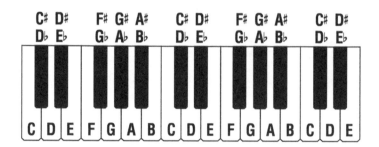

The C located in the middle of the piano keyboard is creatively named **middle C**. Everything above middle C is written in **treble clef** (the curvy symbol on the left side of the example below):

Two mnemonic devices to help you remember note names in **treble clef**:

As a rule, everything below middle C is written in **bass clef** (figure at the left side of the example below):

Two mnemonic devices to help you remember note names in **bass clef**:

The parallel lines upon which notes are written are **staff lines** (the plural is staves). Staves are divided into bars (or measures) by **bar lines**:

In a rehearsal, you will hear, "Let's start at measure (or bar) 16," which makes a good case for writing the measure numbers of your songs into your music – in pencil.

Time signatures, which look a bit like fractions, are located on the left side of the first line of every piece of music. They reappear in a piece only when there is a change of time signature to report. The top number of the time signature tells you how many beats are contained in each measure. The bottom number tells you what kind of beats are in the measures.

Known as **four-four time (4/4)**, this time signature has four quarter-note beats in each measure:

Three-four time (3/4) has three quarter-note beats in each measure:

Four-four time is also known as **common time** and is sometimes indicated with a **C** in place of the time signature.

Reading rhythms within a time signature is simple math. Each measure must add up to the time signature marked at the beginning of the piece. Note values line up as follows:

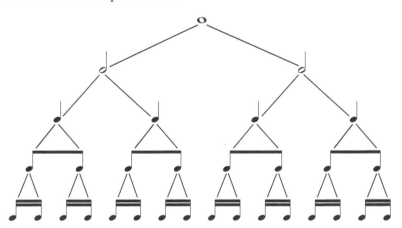

Building Skills

As you get used to practicing every day and learning new music on a regular basis, you will notice you're beginning to develop vocal skills and polish you never had before. This means it's time to focus time and energy on specific skills, both improving the weak areas of your vocal technique and building on your strengths.

Facilitating Facility

Some of the songs you work on will be slow and legato, meant to be crooned. But others will be fast and full of moving notes. Think of "Supercalifragilisticexpialidocious," from Mary Poppins, for instance. Vocal facility, or the ability to sing notes quickly and accurately, is an achievable goal. Like any other technical vocal skill, you must start out slowly and build speed as you become more competent.

To hear how to work on facility, listen to the demo tracks below. As you begin to practice this exercise, you may switch syllables to "lah" or "mah" over time. Once you have really mastered the etude and have it up to a brisk tempo, transpose it higher or lower in your vocal range and master it there as well. By alternating the middle, high, and lower areas of your range with this exercise, you will develop facility and control throughout your range.

 47 & 48 High Voice　　　　 **49 & 50 Low Voice**

Tah　tah　tah　tah　*etc.*

This next exercise uses your digital tuner, or the tuner app on your phone, to work on fine control of a single pitch. You will be rising and sinking just a bit in pitch on a single note. This control is an absolute must as you perform.

Turn on your tuner and pick a pitch somewhere in the middle of your range. Sustain the pitch and work on centering the "needle" on the tuner or tuner app. In other words, bring the pitch in tune with your tuner. Stop and restart the note several times, working on hitting it spot on at the beginning of the note. Once you are comfortable starting the note accurately, work on raising and lowering the "needle" slowly and smoothly. You will be changing the pitch in tiny increments, which is exactly the point. Concentrate on making the "needle" of your tuner move just a little bit and making it move without jumps and lurches. This exercise can be frustrating at first, so don't work on it too much in a single session. (See Video 11 in Chapter 15.)

Arpeggios

Pianos, guitars, organs, and other harmonic instruments (instruments that play more than one note at a time) can play chords. Singers cannot produce more than one note simultaneously, but can sing through chords one note at a time, turning them into arpeggios. Arpeggios pop up in a great deal of the music we sing, outlining harmony and giving a broad, sweeping feeling to the vocal lines of songs.

Listen to Track 51 and Track 52 as the singers move through this arpeggio warm-up. When working on these exercises, always strive for accurate pitch and an even sound from the bottom to the top of the arpeggios. You may extend this exercise either higher or lower on your vocal range for more of a workout from top to bottom.

etc.

Lah _____ lah _____ lah _____ lah.

Cue up the performance of Canadian songwriter Leonard Cohen's secular hymn "Hallelujah" (Track 55). When you first begin working with the accompaniment (Track 56), sing on a single syllable and strive to fit the rhythms precisely to the accompaniment. Add the lyrics after you have mastered the rhythms and pitches.

55 & 56

Hallelujah

Words and Music by Leonard Cohen

Moderately slow, in 2

I've heard there was a
faith was strong but you

se- cret chord _ that Da- vid played, _ and it pleased the Lord, _ but you don't _ real- ly
need- ed proof. _ You saw _ her bath- ing on the roof. Her beau- ty _____ and the

care for mu- sic, _____ do ya? _____ It goes like this: the
moon- light o- ver- threw ya. _____ She tied you to a

fourth, the fifth, the mi- nor fall, _____ the ma- jor lift, _____ the baf- fled king _____ com-
kitch- en chair. She broke your throne; _ she cut your hair. _____ And from your lips _____ she

pos- ing _____ Hal- le- lu- jah. _____
drew the _____ Hal- le- lu- jah. _____

Hal- le- lu- jah, _____ Hal- le- lu- jah, _____ Hal- le-

1.
lu- jah. Your lu-

2.
jah. Hal- le- lu- jah. _____ Hal- le- lu- jah. _____ Hal- le-

lu- jah. _____ Hal- le- lu- jah. _____

Making Music

Have you ever noticed that some performers can absolutely break your heart with a single song? Yet, someone else singing that same song may be only mildly interesting. The reason for the seeming sleight of hand is that generating notes and making music are not the same thing. Reading notes and producing the sounds they indicate is the craft of music making. Taking those notes and creating an interesting performance that's sensitive and meaningful is an art.

Dynamics and phrasing are two closely related key elements in music making. Phrasing is the art of taking a musical line, essentially a string of notes, and giving it shape and direction. Listen to Track 57, in which the singer performs "Scarborough Fair" (see page 5) with no thought whatsoever to phrasing. Then go back to Track 9, where it's sung with gracefully arced phrases. Listen to the second rendition several times. You'll notice that shaping the phrase is a combination of dynamic changes, accents (musical stresses) and a bit of *rubato* (a slight pushing and pulling of the tempo, to create a musical effect).

 57 "Scarborough Fair"

Shaping a Phrase

Say the following sentence aloud with a strong emphasis on a different word each time:

- **I** don't have any idea what you're talking about.
- I don't have **any** idea what you're talking about.
- I **don't** have any idea what you're talking about.
- I don't have any idea what **you're** talking about.
- I don't have any idea **what** you're talking about.

Each time you put the accent on a different word, you change the shape of the phrase. Just as an actor might try out the accent on each possible word to see what effect best suits the meaning of the sentence, a singer might experiment with emphasis on each word, and its corresponding note, in a phrase of music.

Once you've decided which word in the phrase is most important, you can take this a little further by making a ***crescendo*** (a gradual increase in volume) leading up to that note, and a ***diminuendo*** (a gradual decrease in volume) on the notes moving away from the accented note. You can also make the accent sudden, with no *crescendo* leading up to it, or shape that phrase any way that suits your taste.

Many singers mark phrasings in their music with long, arced lines penciled above the music – to indicate where a single phrase begins and ends. *Crescendos* and *diminuendos* are marked below the music with a symbol that looks like a long V, laid on its side. The wide end of the V indicates more volume, the closed point indicates less volume.

crescendo   *diminuendo*

We use Italian words to refer to dynamic levels, or volume levels, within a piece of music. **Piano**, which means "soft," is written with a single **p**. **Forte**, which means loud, is written with a single **f**. To help sort out how loud and soft to make the music, the abbreviations may be doubled or tripled or paired with the letter "m" for the Italian word **mezzo** (middle or medium).

ppp – very, very soft	**mf** – moderately loud
pp – very soft	**f** – loud
p – soft	**ff** – very loud
mp – moderately soft	**fff** – very, very loud

Accents, which indicate a stress on a single note, are indicated with a small sideways V above or below the note. The accent mark looks like a miniature diminuendo mark, which is exactly what it is. The accent mark tells you to add a stress on the beginning of the note.

Music making involves more than just getting louder and softer. It also includes subtle changes in the tempo and rhythm of a piece to help focus the listener on notes or lyrics that are important.

A slight hold on a single note may be indicated with a **tenuto** mark:

A longer hold on a note may be indicated with a **fermata**:

You might also use **rubato**, which is a subtle pushing and pulling of the tempo.

Listen to the demo recording of "Scarborough Fair" (Track 9) again, paying close attention to details of phrasing and dynamics. Then sing along with accompaniment (Track 10), experimenting with your own choices of dynamics, phrasings, and accents. Mark your final choices in the music, in pencil.

Working on a Song

Slow Down!

Take your time learning new songs. Live with the song and what it's saying for a few weeks before you commit to an interpretation. Spend a little time in that delightful stage that finds you humming the song in the car and mumbling the lyrics as you take a walk. The quicker you pick up a song, the quicker you'll forget it. Mastering a new song is like making a great cup of tea – you have to let it steep a while to get the full flavor out of the brew.

Technically Speaking

Lots of the songs you sing will be mostly easy to master, with one or two hard spots tucked in. Your audience doesn't need to know which sections of a song are hardest for you to sing, so make a habit of pulling out those sections and working on them separately from the rest. The easy parts don't need as much as practice as the hard parts. Put parentheses around the tough spots (using a pencil, of course) and spend time in each practice session working on just those marked parts. It's okay to go several days without singing a song straight through, if you're working on the details – in fact, it's recommended!

Listen to the singer in Track 58 working on "Skye Boat Song." You might want to pull out the big leaps and work on those intervals. Singing them slowly and smoothly, alternating with singing them on a short "da" or "pa" syllable, to ensure that you will always hit those notes precisely.

58 Practicing "Skye Boat Song"

Recording yourself in practice sessions, performances, voice lessons and coachings can be a great tool. One thing you will likely notice when you hear yourself on a recording: the big musical moment that felt like such a great expression of emotion will probably sound pretty tame in a replay. Most of us don't make grand, emotional statements on a regular basis in our daily lives. When we're called upon to do that while singing, we're a little uncomfortable letting loose and really going for it. Remember, you want to communicate to the people in the back of the room as well as those in the front. Make sure they all know what you think about the song you're singing. Listen as the singer in Track 59 works to make a crescendo convincing.

59 Practicing "You Raise Me Up"

To get an accurate impression of how you sound on one of your songs, record it, but *don't listen* to the recording for a day or two. If you listen right away, your mind will either hear what you thought you were doing rather than what you were actually doing, or it will hear only the flaws you were aware of as you sang and not the things you did well. Allow some time and then listen critically, thinking about both what you like and what you want to do better. There will be some of both.

It Matters When You Sing

It's not a good idea to leave your practicing for late in the evening. By the end of the day you're tired, so you won't be concentrating nor will you be standing, breathing, and singing your best. It's also not a good idea to roll out of bed in the morning and jump right into practicing. Allow a little time for your body to wake up before singing – perhaps a brisk walk first, to get the blood flowing, and some breakfast, to make sure you're fueled up. Always make sure you're well hydrated, which can be accomplished by drinking plenty of water, herbal tea, or other beverages that won't coat your throat with gooey, dairy residue or a sticky, sugary coating.

Don't Forget to Memorize

Singers memorize their music. Unless you're singing in a church balcony, recording studio, or some other spot where your audience can't see you, you will need to memorize your music.

For singers, memorization involves two elements: the tune and the lyrics. Of the two, the lyrics often pose the bigger challenge. Listen to Track 60 as a singer works to memorize different elements of "Give My Regards to Broadway": first, intoning the text and rhythm, which means singing it on a single pitch, with a metronome; then speaking the lyrics with a metronome; then singing the song slowly and then faster than the marked tempo, always working on fitting lyrics and rhythms precisely in place.

 60 Practicing "Give My Regards to Broadway"

Before you work on a new song, make a road map of it. Does it have verses and a chorus? Is there a bridge in the song that prepares the listener for the return of the main tune? Understanding the map will help you cement the song in your memory. In a ballad, or any song that tells a story, knowing the progression of the story helps a lot in memorizing the lyrics.

Work on the lyrics away from the music. Walking and chanting the lyrics, mentally of course, can be a useful aid. As you walk, your footsteps will fall in an even rhythm you can use as the beat under the lyrics. Write out a road map for "Give My Regards to Broadway," and use the tools in this lesson to work on learning and memorizing the song.

 61 & 62

Give My Regards to Broadway
from LITTLE JOHNNY JONES

Words and Music by George M. Cohan

Dealing with Nerves

We've all seen someone step into the spotlight and freeze, with a deer-in-the-headlights look on his or her face. That's stage fright at its worst. Successful performers learn early on that the same adrenalin that causes stage fright can be a valuable tool, but only if it can be controlled. The adrenalin experienced when stepping in front of an audience is a natural part of performing, and something most people facing an audience experience to some degree. For many musicians, actors, dancers, and public speakers, that adrenalin is an essential part of getting keyed up for a gig, providing an edge of excitement, and heightening focus and energy.

Some performers are cool as cucumbers under pressure. They suffer no physical or mental effects of nervousness, or stage fright. Others, the minority for whom it becomes a serious problem, use hypnosis, therapy, and/or prescription drugs to minimize its effects. But most people who regularly work in front of audiences fall somewhere in the middle of those two extremes: they experience some stage fright and learn to cope with nervousness and its physical effects without extreme measures.

Eliminating Tension

Video 9
Watch Video 9 for some tips on combatting nerves.

Most of the physical jitters that accompany nervousness are the result of tension and lack of oxygen. Knowing what causes those jitters means you can work to avoid them. When you're nervous, you unconsciously begin taking shallow, quick breaths, robbing your body of the oxygen it needs. Lack of oxygen causes muscles to feel weak and tremble, creating wobbling knees, trembling hands and so on. As muscles begin to tremble, your tension level rises, your breathing becomes even shallower, and the effects become even more pronounced.

Video 10
Watch as the singer in Video 10 goes through a series of relaxing exercises to combat the effects of nerves.

Get yourself in front of an audience as often as possible to help master the nerves and adrenalin generated by performing. You can give mock performances in front audiences of family, friends, or colleagues, or perhaps in a school or retirement home. Make sure to schedule these mock or warm-up "gigs" far enough in advance of the actual performance that you leave yourself enough time to work on any musical details you might want to continue polishing. "Warm-up" performances are such a good tool that professional singers and other musicians often perform for friends and colleagues before big concerts or auditions. They deal with nerves too, you know.

Do Your Homework

Remember, a singer's job is to sing. Prepare your material well and then focus on the fact that you have a job to do. As you prepare for the gig, use the warm-up exercises you do in your daily practice: go through them slowly and in the same order you use every day. Observing a familiar routine will focus your mind on the task at hand and help prepare your body to do its best. Bring along the same notebook you use to jot down intrusive thoughts while warming up and practicing – it will help you get control over racing, disorganized thoughts. Preparation and mental focus are your best weapons against stage fright and your best tools for giving a good performance.

Something Familiar

Singing a familiar song, the sort you might sing in the shower or while driving down a country road, can be a great way to quiet performance nerves. Choose one that is calming, not something with a fast tempo or punchy rhythms. Hum or sing through it slowly, breathing deeply and enjoying the feel and the process of singing. For the moment you might use "Scarborough Fair," which you worked on earlier in these lessons.

To develop your interpretation of "You Raise Me Up," listen to the performance on Track 63 before using the accompaniment (Track 64). This is a great song for a direct, heartfelt delivery, and perfect to use as a calming warm-up when you try out the acoustics and sound system in an unfamiliar performance space.

63 & 64

You Raise Me Up

Words and Music by Brendan Graham and Rolf Lovland

Making a Song Your Own

Songs are amazing things – entities really. Each time someone new sings a song, they bring their own life experience and musical abilities to it, interpreting it from their own perspective, and making it something original and different than it was before.

As a person learning to sing today, you have an advantage over previous generations of singers in that you can use the Internet to hear a remarkable amount of music. Search for the song "I Will." You will come up with recordings by Paul McCartney, who wrote it for his then future wife Linda Eastman. Start with McCartney's interpretation of the song and then listen to covers (the industry term for new recordings of a song that's already been recorded) by Alison Krauss, Maureen McGovern, Tim Curry, Hugh Masekela, Ben Taylor, and Diana Ross. Each version brings something different to the music. Keep searching, if you like, and see whose recording you like best.

You too can interpret a song in a way that makes it uniquely yours, but it requires thought and emotional investment, and solid, basic vocal skills. Use the dynamics and phrasing tools from earlier in the book, as well as the "scoop" presented here. But mostly you must use your ears and your musical taste to make a song your own.

The Scoop

The vocal slide, also known as a "scoop," is essentially a glissando between notes or leading into a single note. It is a great interpretive tool to keep handy and to use sparingly. Listen to the opening of Etta James's iconic recording of "At Last" on the Internet for a perfect example of a scoop.

On the tracks referenced below, the singers use an exercise for controlling pitch and nailing the arrival note in a scoop. When you begin singing along, or working with the accompaniment tracks, sing softly so you can hear the pitches clearly and match them perfectly.

 65 & 66 High Voice   **67 & 68 Low Voice**

Once you have mastered the short scoop above, listen to the longer scoops in the tracks referenced below. Again, when you begin working on this exercise yourself, sing softly so that you can hear the pitches in the accompaniment and match them perfectly.

 69 & 70 High Voice   **71 & 72 Low Voice**

Scoops can add color and character to your singing, but must not be used too often. Listen to the entire recording of Etta James singing "At Last," and notice that it is *not* peppered with scoops like the one that creates such an expressive, attention-grabbing opening to the song.

Give It a Try

Now use the Internet to listen to the following recordings of "Georgia on My Mind," paying close attention to the ways in which each singer made the song their own. Listen to the opening bars of each recording a few extra times, while watching the music.

GEORGIA ON MY MIND
Words by Stuart Gorrell
Music by Hoagy Carmichael
Copyright © 1930 by Peermusic III, Ltd.
Copyright Renewed
International Copyright Secured   All Rights Reserved

Ray Charles shortens some notes, scoops a few other notes, adds some ornamental notes and gives the song a wistful, nostalgic feel.

Willie Nelson adds some ornamental notes and sings much of the song in short phrase fragments, as though he is remembering a place from his past and speaking half out loud.

Michael Bublé gives the song a sighing sound, as though he's talking to himself, lost in is thoughts.

Annie Lennox turns the song into a heartfelt wail, making a much bigger sound than most of the other singers who have recorded it. She adds vocal fills and lets her voice break for effect.

Billie Holiday gives the song the feel of a last dance at a big-band club, complete with a satiny, 1940s sound and a nicely percolating rhythm.

Now it's your turn to experiment a bit with the tools you've listened to in the lessons – to make the song "At Last" express your own feelings. Listen to the low-voice demo (Track 73) and to the famous Etta James recording. Then use the accompaniment (Track 74) to start working out your own interpretation. If you're more comfortable singing "At Last" in a higher key, print a copy of the PDF (on MyLibrary) and use the piano accompaniment on Track 75.

 73–75

At Last
from ORCHESTRA WIVES

Lyric by Mack Gordon
Music by Harry Warren

Rules and Tools

Rules

Copyrights

Before you do any buying, borrowing, or photocopying of music (or copying of recordings), you should know that laws exist to protect songwriters and recording artists from having their work duplicated without their permission – in other words, stolen.

When you begin singing gigs, you'll expect to be paid for your efforts. Just as you want remuneration, so do songwriters, lyricists, and recording artists. Copyrights are the rights of the creator or owner of a piece of "intellectual property" (songs, poems, books, plays, etc.) to make and distribute copies of their own work. The copyright symbol looks like this: ©

Printed music is most often copyrighted, as are books, poems, professional photographs, audio recordings, radio and television broadcasts, and motion pictures. Works that were never copyrighted or on which copyrights have expired are in the "public domain" and are free for you to copy and use. However, a song that is in the public domain may be available in several copyrighted arrangements. Make sure you understand the copyright laws concerning the media you intend to copy before you find yourself in trouble. Breaking copyright laws can be quite expensive. Be aware that just because something is posted on Pinterest, Facebook, or elsewhere on the Internet, does not mean it is in the public domain.

Items in the public domain will often bear the following symbol:

Accompanists

Accompanists deserve to be paid. A good accompanist, or more deferentially, "collaborative pianist," is a trained musician who will take the time to learn your music and support your musical choices in performance. Treat these people with respect, ask what they charge for the services you need, and pay them fully and promptly.

Professional Behavior

Showing up right on time for a rehearsal or performance means you're late. Always arrive early for musical commitments and always arrive warmed-up, with music learned and in your hand, dressed appropriately for the event, and ready to work. Regardless of how well you sing, the reputation of being unreliable and/or unprofessional will torpedo your musical aspirations.

Tools

Marking Your Music

Always have a sharpened pencil and an eraser on hand. If your music is on a tablet or dedicated music reader, make sure you know how to mark the music and can save those markings to your device.

Tuner

As we discussed in Lesson 10, a tuner is an essential tool for practicing. It will tell you if your pitch (intonation) drifts as you change dynamics, or as you near the end of a long phrase.

Video 11
Singer working with tuner

Recorder

A device for making sound recordings is a must. Recording yourself and going back to that recording a few hours, or a day, later can reveal all sorts of issues you were not aware of as you sang.

Metronome

The tempo of a piece is often indicated just above the piece's first measure: ♩ = 120. Your metronome will tell you how fast that is and will help you as you work on a piece at a tempo that's slower than that, gradually speeding up to the marked tempo.

Video 12
Singer working on "Give My Regards to Broadway" using a metronome

Speakers

Most of us listen to a lot of music on our computers or other devices. Sadly, tiny speakers on electronic devices, as well as inexpensive, external computer speakers, do not provide much in the way of depth of sound and the performer's musical nuances. Earbuds and headphones limit you to listening passively to a recording, whereas speakers allow you to work with a recording. Make sure you get speakers that will work with your devices, whether through a cable or wireless connection.

FYI: You can now find smartphone apps to cover the functions of metronomes, tuners, and audio recorders.

Apply the various skills and principles you've learned in these lessons to "Cups (When I'm Gone)." The song has its roots in "You're Gonna Miss Me," written in 1928 by A.P Carter, Sara Carter, and Maybelle Carter, members of the Carter Family singing group. On the Internet, you can listen to both contemporary recordings of the song, as well as those going all the way back to the Carter Family. Be sure to search for both of the song's titles.

76 & 77

Cups (When I'm Gone)
from the Motion Picture Soundtrack PITCH PERFECT

Words and Music by A.P. Carter, Luisa Gerstein and Heloise Tunstall-Behrens

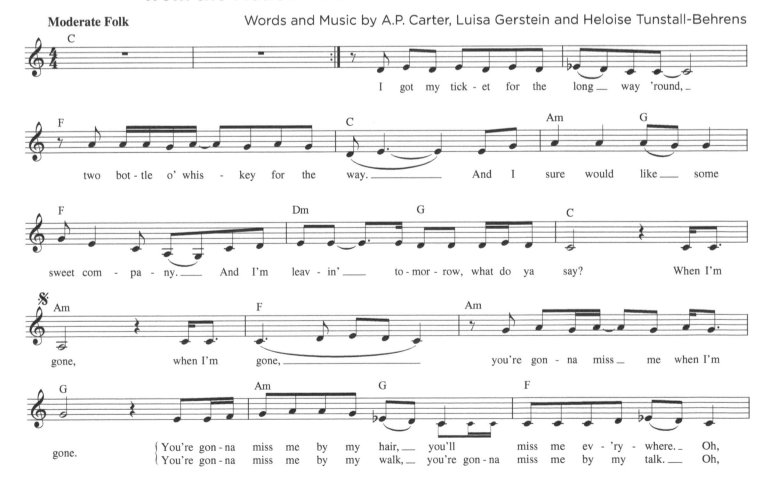

Vocals: Beth Mulkerron & Jesse Weinberg

Piano: J. Mark Baker & Teresa Drews

Video model: Beth Mulkerron

Video voice-overs: Elaine Schmidt

Audio & video recorded at Tanner-Monagle Studios; Milwaukee, WI